Gooseberry Patch®

Our Favorit
Recipes for a Crowd

Copyright 2016, Gooseberry Patch

Make a quick condiment kit for your next backyard barbecue.
Just place salt, pepper, mustard, catsup, flatware and napkins
in an empty cardboard pop carrier...so easy!

Kari's Buffalo Chicken Dip

Serves 12 to 16

2 8-oz. pkgs. cream cheese,
　　softened
1 deli roast chicken, boned
　　and chopped
16-oz. bottle blue cheese
　　salad dressing

1/3 c. hot pepper sauce,
　　or to taste
tortilla chips

Combine all ingredients except tortilla chips in an ungreased
13"x9" baking pan. Bake, uncovered, at 375 degrees for 30 minutes,
or until hot and bubbly. Serve with tortilla chips.

Have a fiesta! After a south-of-the-border dinner, serve up some Mexican "fried" ice cream. Freeze individual scoops of ice cream while dinner's cooking, roll in crushed frosted corn flake cereal and drizzle with honey. Top with a sprinkle of cinnamon, whipped cream and a cherry.

10-Layer Taco Dip

Serves 25

31-oz. can refried beans
2 lbs. ground beef
1-1/4 oz. pkg. taco seasoning mix
8-oz. pkg. cream cheese, softened
16-oz. container sour cream
24-oz. jar salsa
2 to 3 tomatoes, chopped
1 onion, chopped
2 green peppers, chopped

8-oz. pkg. shredded lettuce
8-oz. pkg. shredded Mexican-
blend cheese
2 2-1/4 oz. cans sliced black
olives, drained
Optional: sliced jalapeño peppers,
corn, black beans
tortilla chips

Spread beans in a lightly greased 13"x11" aluminum foil baking pan; set aside. Brown beef in a skillet over medium heat; drain. Add taco seasoning to beef and cook according to package directions. Let cool; spread over bean layer. In a bowl, mix together cream cheese and sour cream; spoon over beef. Top with remaining ingredients except tortilla chips in order given. Arrange jalapeños, corn and black beans over top, if desired. Cover with aluminum foil and refrigerate for at least one hour to overnight. Serve with tortilla chips.

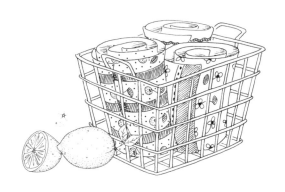

Set out a basket of fingertip towels with sticky,
flavorful ribs or wings. Dampen towels with water and
lemon juice, roll up and microwave until warm.

Little Sugar Piggies

30 hot dogs
2 lbs. bacon
wooden toothpicks

16-oz. pkg. light brown sugar
Optional: 3 to 4 shakes hot pepper
   sauce

Cut hot dogs and bacon slices into 3 to 4 equal pieces each. Wrap each
hot dog piece with a piece of bacon; secure with a toothpick. Transfer
wrapped hot dogs to a slow cooker. Add brown sugar and hot sauce,
if using, to slow cooker. Cover and cook on low setting, stirring
occasionally, for 5 to 6 hours, until bacon is cooked.

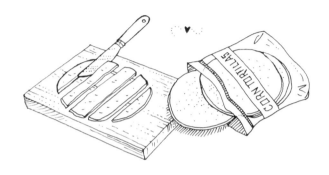

Crunchy tortilla strips are a tasty addition to
southwestern-style soups. Cut corn tortillas into
thin strips, then deep-fry quickly. Drain on paper towels
before sprinkling over bowls of soup. Try red or
blue tortilla chips too.

Nachos for a Crowd

13-1/2 oz. pkg. round tortilla chips
15-oz. can homestyle chili
8-oz. pkg. shredded Mexican-blend cheese
1/2 c. queso sauce
10-oz. pkg. shredded lettuce
1 onion, diced
1 green pepper, chopped
1/2 c. jalapeño pepper, sliced
Optional: 1/2 c. sliced black olives, 4-oz. can diced green chiles
1/2 c. sour cream
1 tomato, diced
2 T. dried chives

Arrange chips on a large microwave-safe plate; set aside. Heat chili in a microwave-safe bowl on high setting for one minute; stir. Microwave for another minute; set aside. Sprinkle tortilla chips with cheese; microwave on high setting for 30 seconds. Spoon chili and queso sauce over cheese; sprinkle with lettuce, onion, green pepper and jalapeño. Top with black olives and green chiles, if using. Add a dollop of sour cream; sprinkle with tomato and chives.

Traveling a distance to your cookout site? Wrap and freeze burgers or marinated meat before packing in your ice chest. The frozen meat will help keep other items cold and will thaw in time for grilling.

Sausage Balls for a Crowd

Makes 3 to 4 dozen

16-oz. pkg. ground pork
   breakfast sausage
1 c. all-purpose flour

16-oz. pkg. shredded sharp
   Cheddar, Pepper Jack or
   mozzarella cheese

Combine all ingredients in a large bowl. Knead together until completely incorporated. Form mixture into one to 1-1/2 inch balls. Place balls on parchment paper-lined baking sheets, one inch apart. Bake at 350 degrees for 15 to 20 minutes, until golden and and sausage is no longer pink. Cool slightly before serving. May be baked, then refrigerated up to one week in a plastic zipping bag and warmed at serving time.

Make assembly part of pizza night fun! Prepare the crust, then set out the sauce, pepperoni, veggies, seasonings and cheese. Let family members add toppings as they like... even little ones can help out. Bake, slice and dinner's ready!

Healthy Jalapeño Poppers

Makes 20 poppers

1 T. olive oil
1/2 lb. ground turkey breast
3/4 c. green pepper, finely
   chopped
1/2 c. onion, finely chopped
1 clove garlic, minced

1/2 c. fat-free cream cheese,
   softened
Greek seasoning to taste
10 jalapeño peppers, halved
   and seeded
Garnish: low-fat Parmesan cheese

Heat oil in a skillet over medium heat. Brown turkey with green pepper, onion and garlic; drain. Transfer turkey mixture to a bowl; blend in cream cheese and seasoning. Add one tablespoon of turkey mixture to each jalapeño half; sprinkle with Parmesan cheese. Transfer filled jalapeños to lightly greased baking sheets. Bake at 425 degrees for 15 to 20 minutes, or until tops are golden.

Start a cooking club with friends! Decide on dishes
ahead of time, then everyone shops for just a part of
the meal. Get together to cook and pack dishes
in freezer containers.

Pineapple Cheese Ball

2 8-oz. pkgs. cream cheese,
   softened
8-oz. can pineapple tidbits,
   drained
2 to 4 T. onion, chopped
1/2 c. green pepper, chopped

1/2 t. salt
Optional: pepper to taste
2 c. chopped pecans or walnuts
snack crackers, pita wedges and
   celery sticks

In a bowl, blend together cream cheese, pineapple, onion, green pepper
and seasonings. Mix well; roll into one or 2 balls. Roll in chopped nuts to
coat. Wrap in plastic wrap; keep refrigerated. Serve with crackers, pita
wedges and celery.

Turn chocolate-dipped strawberries into tasty little footballs!
Pipe melted white chocolate onto strawberries for
the lacing and details...so cute.

Spicy Tailgate Dip

Serves 16 to 20

1 lb. ground pork sausage,
   browned and drained
2 8-oz. pkgs. cream cheese,
   cubed

10-oz. can diced tomatoes with
   green chiles
corn chips

Combine all ingredients except chips in a slow cooker. Cover and cook on low setting for one to 2 hours, until heated through and cream cheese is melted. Serve with corn chips.

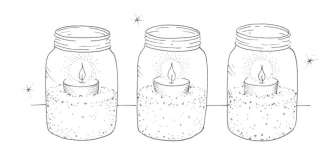

Getting together outside? Set tea lights inside drinking glasses and line up down the center of the table...their flame won't go out!

Iced Coffee Punch

Makes 50 servings

1 c. instant coffee granules
2-1/2 c. sugar
4 c. boiling water
1/2 gal. vanilla ice cream
1/2 gal. chocolate ice cream
1/2 gal. coffee ice cream
3 gals. milk
16-oz. container frozen whipped
   topping, thawed
Garnish: chocolate sprinkles

Dissolve coffee granules and sugar in boiling water; chill. Divide cooled
coffee mixture, ice creams and milk between two 3-gallon punch bowls.
Top punch with whipped topping, spreading with a spatula. Garnish with
sprinkles. Serve immediately.

Jams and preserves keep well, so pick up a few jars of local specialties like beach plum, peach or boysenberry on family vacations. Later, use them to bake up jam cakes or thumbprint cookies...the flavors will bring back happy memories!

Country Morning Coffee Cake

Serves 18 to 20

1 c. margarine, softened
2 c. sugar
4 eggs, beaten
2 c. sour cream
4 c. all-purpose flour

2 t. baking soda
2 t. baking powder
1 t. salt
2 t. vanilla extract

Combine margarine, sugar, eggs and sour cream in a large bowl. Stir in remaining ingredients; mix thoroughly. Pour into a greased 15"x10" jelly-roll pan; sprinkle with Cinnamon-Pecan Topping. Bake at 350 degrees for 25 minutes, until a toothpick tests clean. Cut into squares.

Cinnamon-Pecan Topping:

2/3 c. brown sugar, packed
1/2 c. sugar

1/2 c. chopped pecans
2 t. cinnamon

Use a fork to mix all ingredients together.

No need to slice and serve...bake a quiche in
muffin or custard cups for oh-so simple individual servings.
When making minis, reduce the baking time by about 10 minutes,
and slide a toothpick into each to check for doneness.

Scrambled Eggs for a Crowd

Serves 10 to 12

2 doz. eggs
1 c. half-and-half
1/2 t. salt
1/2 t. pepper
2 c. cooked ham, diced

1 T. butter
1/2 c. red pepper, chopped
1/2 c. green onion, chopped
1/2 c. sliced mushrooms
1 c. shredded Cheddar cheese

In a large bowl, whisk together eggs, half-and-half and seasonings. Spray a slow cooker with non-stick vegetable spray; pour mixture into slow cooker. Top with ham. Cover and cook on high setting for one hour, stirring after 30 minutes. Cover and cook an additional 40 to 50 minutes, stirring every 10 minutes, until eggs are moist and almost set. In a skillet, melt butter over medium heat; add vegetables. Sauté for 5 minutes, stirring occasionally, until tender. Fold vegetable mixture and cheese into eggs. Cover and let stand several minutes, until cheese melts. Serve immediately, or turn to low setting and hold up to one hour.

Spread some maple butter on fresh pancakes or biscuits.
Just combine 1/2 cup softened butter with 3/4 cup maple
syrup and beat until fluffy...yum!

Jumbo Cinnamon Rolls

Makes 12 to 15 rolls

1 T. active dry yeast
1/4 c. warm water
1/4 c. instant vanilla pudding mix
1 c. milk
1/4 c. oil
1 egg, beaten

4 c. all-purpose flour
2 T. sugar
1/2 t. salt
1-1/2 T. cinnamon
1/2 c. brown sugar, packed
16-oz. can vanilla frosting

In a large bowl, dissolve yeast in very warm water, about 110 to 115 degrees. In a separate bowl, combine dry pudding mix, milk, oil and egg. Add pudding mixture to yeast mixture. In another bowl, sift together flour, sugar and salt. Add pudding mixture to flour mixture; stir until mixed well and dough forms. Transfer dough to a lightly floured surface; knead for 4 minutes. Place in a greased bowl; let rise, covered, for one hour. Meanwhile, combine cinnamon and brown sugar in a bowl. Roll dough out into a 13-inch by 10-inch rectangle; evenly sprinkle with cinnamon mixture. Roll up dough, starting at a long edge; slice into 12 to 15 rolls. Let rolls rise until double in bulk, about one hour. Transfer rolls to lightly greased baking sheets and bake at 350 degrees for about 15 minutes, until golden. Spread each roll with frosting.

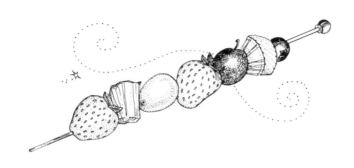

A fresh brunch side dish...fruit kabobs! Just slide pineapple chunks, apple slices, grapes, orange wedges and strawberries onto a wooden skewer. Easy to make for a crowd, and no plate required.

Grandma Retha's Rhubarb Muffins

Makes 12 to 15 muffins

1 c. brown sugar, packed
1 egg, beaten
1 c. buttermilk
1/2 c. oil
2 t. vanilla extract
1-1/2 c. rhubarb, diced
Optional: 1/2 c. chopped walnuts

2-1/2 c. all-purpose flour
1 t. baking powder
1 t. baking soda
1/2 t. salt
1 t. butter, melted
1/2 c. sugar
1 t. cinnamon

In a large bowl, combine brown sugar, egg, buttermilk, oil and vanilla; mix well. Stir in rhubarb and nuts, if using. In a separate bowl, combine flour, baking powder, baking soda and salt; stir into rhubarb mixture. Spoon into 12 to 15 greased muffin tins, filling 2/3 full. Stir together melted butter, sugar and cinnamon; sprinkle over muffins. Bake at 350 degrees for 20 to 25 minutes.

Bring out Mom's vintage china for easy entertaining.
Use the bowls for soup suppers, the teacups for dessert
get-togethers and even set out muffins on the turkey platter!

Texas-Style Sausage Muffins

Makes one dozen

1/2 lb. ground pork sausage
1/3 c. green onion, chopped
1-1/2 c. biscuit baking mix
1-1/2 t. brown sugar, packed

1/2 t. dry mustard
1/4 t. cayenne pepper
2/3 c. milk
1/2 c. shredded Cheddar cheese

Cook and stir sausage and onion in a skillet over medium heat until browned; drain on paper towels and set aside. Mix together biscuit mix, brown sugar, mustard and cayenne pepper in a bowl. Stir in sausage mixture, milk and cheese until just blended. Fill 12 greased muffin cups 2/3 full. Bake at 375 degrees for 20 to 25 minutes, until golden.

Most muffin batters can be stirred up the night before, and can even be scooped into muffin cups. Simply cover and refrigerate...in the morning, pop them in the oven. Your family will love waking up to the sweet smell of muffins baking!

Cheesy Sesame Seed Muffins

Makes one dozen

2 T. butter, divided
1/2 c. onion, chopped
1-1/2 c. biscuit baking mix
1 c. sharp American cheese,
    shredded and divided

1 egg, beaten
1/2 c. milk
1 T. sesame seed, toasted

Melt one tablespoon butter in a skillet over medium heat. Add onion; stir constantly until tender, about 3 minutes. Combine onion, biscuit mix and 1/2 cup cheese in a large bowl. In a separate bowl, combine egg and milk; add to onion mixture, stirring just until moistened. Spoon batter into 12 lightly greased muffin cups, filling 1/2 full. Sprinkle with remaining cheese and sesame seed; dot with remaining butter. Bake at 400 degrees for 13 minutes, or until golden. Remove from pan immediately and serve warm.

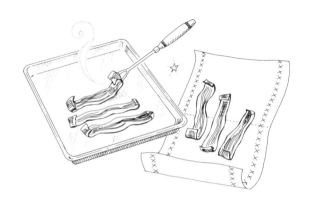

To prepare crispy bacon easily, try baking it in the oven. Place bacon slices on a broiler pan, place the pan in the oven and turn the temperature to 400 degrees. Bake for 12 to 15 minutes, turn bacon over and bake for another 8 to 10 minutes.

Kathy's Bacon Popovers

Makes one dozen

2 eggs
1 c. milk
1 T. oil
1 c. all-purpose flour

1/4 t. salt
3 slices bacon, crisply cooked
    and crumbled

Whisk together eggs, milk and oil. Beat in flour and salt just until smooth. Fill 12 greased and floured muffin cups 2/3 full with batter. Sprinkle bacon over batter. Bake at 400 degrees for 25 to 30 minutes, or until puffed and golden. Serve warm.

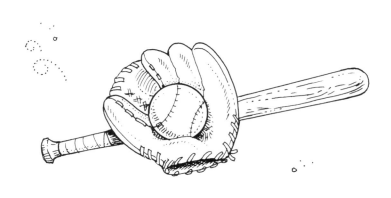

The two most important things in life are
good friends and a strong bullpen.

–Bob Lemon

Anytime Cheesy Biscuits

Makes about 1-1/2 dozen

2 c. biscuit baking mix
1/2 c. shredded Cheddar cheese
2/3 c. milk

1/4 c. butter, melted
1/4 t. garlic powder

Combine biscuit mix, cheese and milk together. Stir until a soft dough forms; beat vigorously for 30 seconds. Drop dough by rounded tablespoonfuls onto an ungreased baking sheet; bake at 450 degrees until golden, about 8 to 10 minutes. Whisk butter and garlic powder together; spread over warm biscuits.

Herbed bread dipping oil is simple to make. Warm together one cup light olive oil and a couple sprigs of fresh rosemary, oregano or thyme. Cool slightly and pour into saucers... perfect for dipping slices of warm crusty bread.

Hoosier Grilled Tenderloin

7-lb. beef tenderloin
1/2 c. butter, melted and cooled
8-oz. bottle Italian salad dressing

4-oz. jar minced garlic
12-oz. bottle dark molasses,
   divided

Place beef in a large plastic zipping bag; set aside. Combine butter, salad dressing and garlic; pour over beef and refrigerate overnight. Remove beef from bag; discard marinade. Brush beef with molasses and place on a preheated grill. Brush with molasses 2 to 3 times during grilling. Grill over medium-high heat for 4 to 6 minutes on each side, or to desired doneness. Slice to serve.

Favorite Ham Casserole

2 c. cooked ham
3 c. elbow macaroni
can crm mushroom soup
3/4 c shredded cheddar
3/4 c milk
bread crumbs

Having a potluck party? Ask everyone ahead of time to share the recipe they'll be bringing. Make copies of all the recipes and staple into a booklet...a thoughtful party souvenir!

Taco Lasagna

Makes 2 pans; each serves 8

2 lbs. ground beef chuck
2 1-1/4 oz. pkgs. taco
   seasoning mix
4 egg whites, beaten
2 15-oz. containers ricotta cheese

24 lasagna noodles, cooked
2 16-oz. pkgs. finely shredded
   Colby Jack cheese
2 24-oz. jars salsa

Brown beef; drain. Stir in taco seasoning, adding a small amount of water if a thinner sauce is desired. Remove from heat. In a bowl, combine egg whites and ricotta cheese until well blended. Lightly spray two 13"x9" baking pans with non-stick vegetable spray. In each pan, layer 4 noodles, 3/4 cup cheese mixture, half of beef mixture and 1-1/3 cups shredded cheese. Next, layer each casserole with 4 noodles, 3/4 cup cheese mixture, remaining beef mixture, 1-1/2 cups salsa and 1-1/3 cups shredded cheese. Bake at 350 degrees for about 40 minutes, until hot and bubbly. Let stand for 10 minutes before serving.

When shopping for cloth napkins, be sure to pick up
an extra one...use it to wrap around a flower pot, pitcher
or pail and you'll always have a matching centerpiece.

Cherry-Glazed Baked Ham

Serves 15 to 20

12 to 15-lb. fully-cooked
   bone-in ham
1 t. allspice

2-ltr. bottle cola
3/4 c. cherry jelly
1/4 c. orange juice

Place ham fat-side up in a shallow roasting pan. With a knife, score a diamond pattern into top of ham. Sprinkle with allspice; rub into ham. Pour cola into pan. Bake at 325 degrees for one hour and 15 minutes, basting with pan juices every 15 minutes. Combine jelly and orange juice in a saucepan over medium heat, stirring until melted. Brush ham with jelly glaze. Bake for an additional 15 to 30 minutes, basting with pan juices every 15 minutes, until a meat thermometer inserted into the thickest part of ham registers 140 degrees. Remove ham from oven; let stand 30 minutes before carving.

Bake a panful of roasted vegetables alongside a casserole. Slice, cube or trim zucchini, cauliflower, sweet peppers, mushrooms, asparagus and other veggies of your choice. Toss with olive oil and spread on a jelly-roll pan. Bake at 350 degrees for 30 to 35 minutes, stirring occasionally, until tender.

Chicken Noodle Casserole *Serves 12*

1/4 c. butter
1 onion, chopped
1 green pepper, chopped
5 to 6 stalks celery, chopped
4-oz. jar diced pimentos, drained
4-oz. can diced green chiles
10-3/4 oz. can cream of
    mushroom soup

3 9-3/4 oz. cans chicken, drained
    slightly
12-oz. pkg. elbow macaroni,
    cooked
12-oz. pkg. shredded Mexican-
    blend cheese, divided

Melt butter in a Dutch oven over medium heat. Add onion, green pepper, celery, pimentos and chiles; sauté until tender. Stir in soup and chicken with liquid. Simmer for 10 minutes. Spread macaroni in a lightly greased 13"x9" baking pan; sprinkle with half the cheese. Spread chicken mixture over cheese; stir gently. Sprinkle with remaining cheese. Bake, uncovered, at 350 degrees for 30 minutes, until cheese is bubbly and golden. Let stand for 5 minutes before serving.

When you put away groceries, be sure to label any ingredients that are intended for dinner...that way, Wednesday's supper won't turn into Tuesday's after-school snack! Set aside cubed cheese, veggies and fruit labeled "OK for snacking" to tame appetites.

Mama Ricciuti's Spaghetti Gravy   *Serves 10 to 15*

2 T. olive oil
2-lb. pork shoulder roast
2 lbs. hot Italian ground pork
    sausage
8 cloves garlic, coarsely chopped
1/2 c. red wine or beef broth
4 28-oz. cans tomato sauce

18-oz. can tomato paste
4 plum tomatoes, chopped
salt and pepper to taste
2 16-oz. pkgs. spaghetti,
    cooked
Garnish: grated Parmesan cheese

Heat oil in a large saucepan over medium heat. Add pork roast, sausage
and garlic. Cook until roast and sausage are browned; drain. Add wine
or broth; cook for one minute and set aside. Combine tomato sauce and
paste in a Dutch oven; stir in tomatoes. Add meat mixture, remaining
wine or broth, salt and pepper. Simmer over medium heat for 2 to
2-1/2 hours. Remove pork roast to a plate and shred with 2 forks.
Return meat to pan and stir gently. Spoon over hot pasta; garnish with
Parmesan cheese.

A pizza cutter makes quick work of dividing up casserole servings while the casserole is still in the baking pan!

Crowd-Size Pizza Hot Dish

Makes 30 servings

6 c. elbow macaroni, uncooked
3 lbs. ground beef
1 onion, chopped
3 15-oz. cans tomato sauce
1-1/2 T. salt
1 T. pepper
1 T. dried oregano
2 t. garlic powder
3 eggs, beaten
1-1/2 c. milk
2 16-oz. pkgs. shredded Cheddar
  cheese

Cook macaroni according to package directions; drain. Place in a large bowl and set aside. In a skillet over medium heat, brown beef and onion together; drain. Stir in tomato sauce and seasonings; blend well. Simmer for 5 to 10 minutes, stirring occasionally. Whisk eggs and milk together; blend into macaroni. Add beef mixture and stir well. Transfer into 2 greased 13"x9" baking pans. Top with cheese. Bake, uncovered, at 350 degrees for 20 minutes, until heated through. Let stand 10 minutes before cutting.

An ice cream social is made for kids big or little!
So easy to plan, it's a get-together kids of all ages
can set up and enjoy with family & friends.

Bubbly Tomato Bake for a Crowd

Serves 12 to 16

12 refrigerated southern-style
   biscuits
5 to 6 tomatoes, thinly sliced
1/4 c. fresh basil, chopped
salt and pepper to taste

1/4 c. plus 2 T. green onion,
   sliced
1-1/4 c. mayonnaise
8-oz. pkg. shredded Monterey
   Jack cheese

Place biscuits in a lightly greased 13"x9" baking pan. Flatten biscuits and pinch seams together to seal. Arrange tomatoes on top of dough. Sprinkle with basil, salt and pepper; top with green onion. In a bowl, mix together mayonnaise and cheese. Spoon mayonnaise mixture evenly over all, completely covering tomatoes. Bake, uncovered, at 425 degrees for 12 to 15 minutes, or until heated through and crust is golden. Let stand 15 minutes before cutting into squares.

Food for friends doesn't have to be fancy. Your guests
will be thrilled with old-fashioned comfort foods. Let everyone
help themselves from big platters set right on the table...
they'll love it!

Creamed Chicken For a Crowd

Serves 12 to 15

8 boneless, skinless chicken
    breasts, cubed
1 t. salt
1/2 t. pepper
2 to 4 T. olive oil, divided
2 white onions, chopped

6 carrots, peeled and thinly sliced
2 c. chicken broth, divided
2 to 3 sprigs fresh thyme
1/3 c. butter, softened
3 T. all-purpose flour
12 to 15 baked biscuits, split

Season chicken with salt and pepper. Heat one tablespoon oil in a skillet over medium heat. Working in batches, cook chicken just until golden on all sides, adding another tablespoon of oil if needed. Remove chicken to a platter; set aside. Add remaining oil to skillet; cook onions in oil until translucent and lightly golden. Add chicken, carrots and one cup broth to onions. Stir gently and spoon chicken mixture into a lightly greased large slow cooker. Place thyme sprigs on top. Cover and cook on low setting for 5 to 6 hours, until chicken is nearly done. Discard thyme. In a small bowl, blend butter and flour. Add butter mixture and remaining broth to slow cooker; cook and stir until thickened. Increase heat to high; cover and cook for 30 minutes. Season with additional salt and pepper, if desired. To serve, ladle creamed chicken over split biscuits.

Choose russet potatoes for casserole dishes...they're the best potato for baking. You'll need about 3 medium russets to equal one pound, or approximately 3-1/2 cups chopped potatoes.

Pierogie Casserole

4 onions, chopped
6 T. butter, divided
6 c. potatoes, peeled and boiled
1/2 c. chicken broth
1/2 to 1 c. milk
salt and pepper to taste
2 eggs, beaten
1/4 c. shredded Cooper or
    Colby cheese
1/4 to 1/2 c. shredded Cheddar
    cheese
16-oz. pkg. mafalda pasta,
    cooked

Sauté onions in 2 tablespoons butter; set aside. Mash potatoes with broth, milk, remaining butter, salt and pepper. Add eggs and cheeses; mix well. Layer pasta, potatoes and onions in a greased 13"x9" baking pan. Bake, uncovered, at 350 degrees for 30 minutes.

Use square plastic freezer containers...they take up less room
in your freezer than round ones. To squeeze in even more,
ladle prepared food into plastic zipping bags, seal and
press flat. When frozen, they'll stack easily.

Mac & Cheese Nuggets

Makes 4 dozen

1/4 c. grated Parmesan cheese, divided
1-1/2 T. butter
2 T. all-purpose flour
3/4 c. milk
1-1/4 c. shredded Cheddar cheese

1/4 lb. American cheese slices, chopped
1 egg yolk, beaten
1/4 t. paprika
8-oz. pkg. elbow macaroni, cooked

Lightly grease 48 mini muffin cups. Sprinkle with 2 tablespoons Parmesan cheese, tapping out excess. Melt butter in a large saucepan over medium heat. Stir in flour; cook for 2 minutes. Whisk in milk until boiling, about 5 minutes. Add Cheddar and American cheeses; remove from heat and stir until smooth. Whisk in egg yolk and paprika; fold in macaroni until well coated. Spoon rounded tablespoons of mixture into prepared tins; sprinkle with remaining Parmesan. Bake at 425 degrees until hot and golden, about 10 minutes. Cool for 5 minutes; carefully transfer to a serving plate.

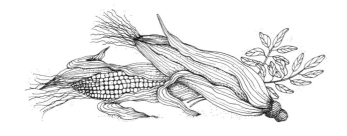

Freeze summer corn to enjoy this winter. Place unhusked ears of corn in a brown grocery bag, roll down and secure the top with a rubber band, place the bags on a shelf in your freezer. When ready to use, let corn thaw enough to husk and prepare in boiling water as your normally would.

Cheesy Corn for a Crowd

Serves 15 to 18

4 15-1/4 oz. cans corn,
    drained
4 15-oz. cans creamed corn
4 eggs, beaten
8-oz. pkg. shredded Cheddar
    cheese
8-oz. pkg. shredded
    mozzarella cheese
2 8-1/2 oz. pkgs. corn muffin
    mix
16-oz. container French
    onion dip

Combine all ingredients except dip in a lightly greased slow cooker. Stir dip into corn mixture. Cover and cook on high setting for 4-1/2 hours, or on low setting for 9 hours.

Whenever grilling chicken for dinner, toss a few extra chicken breasts on the grill. Sliced and refrigerated, they can be served another day in quesadillas, tacos or burritos for an easy meal with fresh-grilled flavor.

Paula's Twice-Baked Potatoes

6 potatoes
1/4 c. butter, softened
1/2 c. milk
1 onion, finely chopped
6 slices bacon, crisply cooked
    and crumbled

1 t. salt
1/2 t. pepper
1-1/2 c. shredded Cheddar
    cheese, divided
Optional; sour cream, chopped
    fresh chives

Bake potatoes at 375 degrees for one hour, or until tender; cool. Cut each potato in half lengthwise and scoop out insides, leaving a thin shell. Mash potato pulp with butter in a bowl. Add milk, onion, bacon, salt, pepper and one cup cheese and mix well. Spoon mixture into potato shells and place on a lightly greased baking sheet. Bake at 375 degrees for 25 minutes. Top with remaining 1/2 cup cheese; bake an additional 5 minutes, or until cheese melts. Garnish with sour cream and chopped fresh chives, if desired.

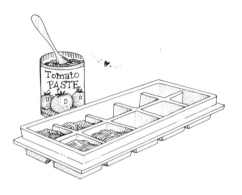

If a recipe calls for just a partial can of tomato paste,
freeze the rest in ice cube trays, then pop out and store in
a freezer bag. Frozen cubes can be dropped into simmering
soups or stews for added flavor...easy!

Icebox Mashed Potatoes

Makes 10 to 12 servings

5 lbs. baking potatoes, peeled
   and halved
2 t. chicken bouillon granules
1/2 t. garlic salt
16-oz. container low-fat
   sour cream

8-oz. pkg. reduced-fat
   cream cheese
2 t. onion powder
2 t. salt
1/4 t. pepper
2 T. butter, sliced

Cover potatoes with water in a deep stockpot; add bouillon and garlic salt. Bring to a boil over high heat; cook until potatoes are tender, about 20 minutes. Remove from heat; drain into a colander. Return potatoes to the same pot and mash. Add remaining ingredients except butter; mix well. Spoon potatoes into a greased 13"x9" baking pan; dot with butter. Cool slightly; cover with plastic wrap and refrigerate up to 3 days. To serve, let stand at room temperature for 30 minutes. Uncover; bake at 350 degrees for 40 minutes. If top browns too quickly, cover with aluminum foil for the last 10 minutes.

Take a little time to share family traditions with your kids
or grandkids! A cherished family recipe can be a great
conversation starter at dinner.

Granny's Cornbread Dressing

Serves 12 to 14

6-1/4 c. cornbread, crumbled
2-1/2 c. chicken broth
1/2 c. butter, melted
1/2 c. onion, chopped
1-1/4 c. celery, chopped

3 T. oil
1 t. seasoned salt
1 t. pepper
5 t. dried sage, or more to taste
3 to 4 eggs, well beaten

In a large bowl, combine cornbread, broth and butter. Mix well and set aside. In a skillet over medium heat, sauté onion and celery in oil until softened, 4 to 5 minutes. Add onion mixture to cornbread mixture along with seasonings; mix well. Let stand for 15 minutes. Fold eggs into cornbread mixture; transfer to a greased 2-quart casserole dish. Bake, uncovered, at 375 degrees for 50 to 65 minutes, until top is golden.

Before marinating chicken, pour some marinade into a plastic squeeze bottle for easy basting...how clever!

Dijon-Ginger Carrots

Makes 10 to 12 servings

12 carrots, peeled and sliced
1/2 c. brown sugar, packed
1 t. fresh ginger, peeled and
    minced

1/3 c. Dijon mustard
1/2 t. salt
1/8 t. pepper

Combine all ingredients in a slow cooker. Cover and cook on high setting for 2 to 3 hours, until carrots are tender, stirring twice during cooking.

For a new twist, substitute packaged stuffing mix for bread crumbs in meatball or meatloaf recipes.

Grandpa Jim's Potatoes

8 to 10 potatoes, peeled, cooked
    and mashed
12-oz. pkg. bacon, crisply cooked
    and crumbled

8-oz. pkg. shredded Cheddar
    cheese
1-1/4 c. ranch salad dressing

Mix all ingredients together in a large bowl. Spoon into a lightly greased 13"x9" baking pan. Bake, uncovered, at 375 degrees for 30 minutes, until heated through.

Make your own seasoning mixes! If you have a favorite busy-day recipe that calls for lots of different herbs or spices, measure them out into several small plastic zipping bags and label. Later, when time is short, just tip a bag into the cooking pot.

Southwest Potato Skins

Makes 12 servings

6 potatoes
1 lb. ground beef
1/2 c. onion, chopped
1 t. salt
1 t. pepper
1-1/4 oz. pkg. taco seasoning mix

2 12-oz. pkgs. shredded
  Cheddar cheese
12-oz. pkg. shredded mozzarella
  cheese, divided
Garnish: fresh chives, bacon bits,
  sour cream

Bake potatoes at 375 degrees for one hour, or until potatoes are tender.
Cut in half lengthwise and scoop out center of each potato, leaving
1/4-inch around edges. Save centers of potatoes for another recipe.
In a large skillet, brown ground beef with onion, salt and pepper; drain.
Add taco seasoning and simmer. Place potato halves in a greased
15"x12" baking pan. Sprinkle with half of Cheddar cheese and all of
beef mixture; top with mozzarella and remaining Cheddar cheese.
Broil 3 to 4 inches from heat source until cheese is bubbly. Top with
chives, bacon bits and sour cream.

Assemble a favorite casserole the night before...in the morning, just pop it in the oven. What a time-saver!

Homestyle Shells & Cheese

Makes 10 to 12 servings

16-oz. pkg. medium shell
   macaroni, uncooked
16-oz. container sour cream
16-oz. container cottage cheese
1 bunch green onions, minced
1 egg, beaten
2 c. shredded Colby Jack cheese

2 c. shredded sharp Cheddar
   cheese
salt and pepper to taste
1/2 c. butter, melted and divided
1 c. Italian-flavored dry bread
   crumbs

Cook macaroni according to package directions; drain and set aside. Meanwhile, in a bowl, mix together sour cream, cottage cheese, onions and egg. Stir in cheeses, salt and pepper; add cooked macaroni and mix well. Coat a 13"x9" baking pan with 2 tablespoons melted butter. Spread mixture evenly in pan. Toss remaining butter with bread crumbs and sprinkle over top. Bake, uncovered, at 350 degrees for 30 to 40 minutes, until cheese is bubbly and bread crumbs are golden.

If an old recipe calls for a cup of sour milk, just stir
a teaspoon of white vinegar into a cup of fresh milk
and let it stand for a few minutes.

Potato Salad for a Crowd

Makes 25 to 30 servings

4 c. mayonnaise-type salad
   dressing
1/4 c. mustard
1 c. sweet pickle relish
1/3 c. white vinegar
1/4 c. sugar
1 T. seafood seasoning

1 t. salt
7 lbs. potatoes, peeled, cubed
   and boiled
8 eggs, hard-boiled, peeled
   and diced
1 yellow onion, finely diced
4-oz. jar diced pimentos, drained

Mix together salad dressing, mustard, relish, vinegar, sugar and
seasonings in a very large bowl. Add potatoes; use a potato masher or
pastry blender to mash potatoes. Stir in remaining ingredients. Chill for
one to 2 hours before serving.

Seed a cucumber in seconds! Cut it in half lengthwise and run a spoon down the center, scooping out the seeds.

Sweet & Tangy Cucumbers

Makes 12 to 15 servings

2 c. sugar
1 c. white vinegar
1 to 2 onions, thinly sliced

10 to 12 cucumbers, peeled and
thinly sliced

Whisk together sugar and vinegar until sugar is dissolved. Toss with remaining ingredients. Refrigerate until ready to serve.

Herbs are happy growing in a sunny windowsill. Tuck them
into Grandma's teacups or cream pitchers for a fresh look...
a clever way to keep them right at your fingertips while cooking!

Patty's Must-Have Salad

Makes 18 to 20 servings

1 head cauliflower, chopped
2 bunches broccoli, chopped
3 stalks celery, sliced
1 onion, finely chopped

1-1/2 c. shredded Cheddar cheese
1 lb. bacon, crisply cooked and
    crumbled

Mix all ingredients in a large bowl. Pour dressing over vegetables; toss until well coated.

Dressing:

3/4 c. sour cream
1-1/2 c. mayonnaise-type
    salad dressing
1/2 t. lemon juice

1/2 t. salt
1-1/2 t. dill weed
1-1/2 t. sugar

Stir together all ingredients until well blended and smooth.

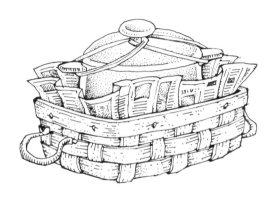

When toting a slow-cooker dish to a potluck, wrap a rubber band around one handle, bring it up over the lid and secure it over the other handle...the lid stays on nice and tight!

Slow-Cooked Baked Beans

Makes 15 to 20 servings

1 lb. bacon, crisply cooked
   and crumbled
2 16-oz. cans pork & beans
16-oz. jar baked beans
15-oz. can kidney beans, drained
   and rinsed
1 c. brown sugar, packed

14-1/2 oz. can lima beans,
   drained and rinsed
2 T. onion, chopped
1/2 c. water
1/2 t. garlic powder
1/2 t. salt

Combine all ingredients in a slow cooker; stir to mix well. Cover and cook on high setting until bubbly, about 1-1/2 hours. Reduce setting to low; cook, covered, for 2 hours. Uncover; return setting to high and cook for an additional hour.

Perfect pasta! Fill a large pot with water and bring to a rolling boil. Add a tablespoon of salt, if desired. Stir in pasta, return to a rolling boil. Boil, uncovered, for the time suggested on package. There's no need to add oil...frequent stirring will keep pasta from sticking together.

Granny's Macaroni Salad

Serves 15 to 20

48-oz. pkg. small macaroni shells,
    uncooked
8-oz. pkg. pasteurized process
    cheese, cubed
1 green pepper, chopped

1 cucumber, shredded
4 to 5 carrots, peeled and
    shredded
2 tomatoes, chopped

Cook macaroni according to package directions. Drain and rinse with cold water. In a large serving bowl, mix cheese and vegetables together; add macaroni. Toss together. Add dressing and mix well. Chill 8 hours to overnight to allow flavors to combine.

Dressing:

2 c. mayonnaise-style salad
    dressing
2 T. sugar

2 T. vinegar
1 T. mustard

Mix together in a small bowl.

For the healthiest meals, choose from a rainbow of colors...
red beets, orange sweet potatoes, yellow summer squash,
dark green kale and Brussels sprouts, purple eggplant and
blueberries. Even white cauliflower offers valuable nutrients.
So fill your plate and eat up!

Quick & Easy Vegetable Salad

Serves 15 to 20

2 15-1/4 oz. cans petite peas,
   drained
2 14-1/2 oz. cans green beans,
   drained
2 15-oz. cans shoepeg corn,
   drained
6 green onions, thinly sliced

4-oz. jar diced pimentoes
1 c. celery, chopped
1 c. sugar
1 c. white vinegar
1 c. oil
salt and pepper to taste

Combine all vegetables in a large bowl; set aside. Mix together sugar, vinegar and oil; pour over vegetables and stir. Add salt and pepper; cover and refrigerate overnight.

Make your own fresh-tasting tomato juice fast! Combine one part tomato paste to 3 parts cold water...add just enough water to suit your taste. Combine in blender until smooth and creamy, add salt and pepper as desired.

Country Club Salad

1-lb. pkg. bacon, crisply cooked
   and crumbled
1 head cauliflower, chopped

1 bunch romaine lettuce, torn
2 heads iceberg lettuce, torn
1 c. crumbled blue cheese

Toss all ingredients together in a large serving bowl; cover and refrigerate until chilled. Pour dressing on top before serving; refrigerating any excess dressing for later use. Toss gently.

Dressing:

1 c. cider vinegar
2 c. sugar
1 T. dry mustard

2 T. garlic powder
1/4 c. egg substitute
3 c. corn oil

Whisk all ingredients together.

Freeze this summer's fresh basil to enjoy it all year long.
Combine 1/4 cup olive oil with 2 cups packed basil leaves in a food
processor. Pulse until finely chopped, spoon into an ice cube tray
and freeze. Place in a plastic freezer bag...great for
flavoring soups, sauces and salad dressings.

Dilly Macaroni Salad

Makes 20 to 25 servings

2 12-oz. pkgs. elbow macaroni,
    uncooked
10 to 12 eggs, hard-boiled, peeled
    and diced
6 to 7 dill pickle spears, diced
1/2 to 1 c. dill pickle juice
15-oz. can sliced black olives,
    drained

1-1/2 c. mayonnaise
1/3 c. mustard
5 T. dill weed
2 T. dried, minced onion
1 T. garlic salt
2 t. seasoned salt
salt and pepper to taste

Cook macaroni according to package directions; drain and rinse with cold water. Combine macaroni and remaining ingredients in a large bowl; sauce will be thin. Cover and refrigerate for at least 4 hours. Stir again before serving.

For a special touch when serving seafood, wrap lemon halves
in cheesecloth, tie with a colorful ribbon and set one on each plate.
Guests can squeeze the lemon over their dishes...
the cheesecloth prevents squirting and catches seeds.

Seafood Salad for a Crowd

Serves 15

3 8-oz. pkgs. cooked frozen
    shrimp, thawed
2 lbs. imitation crabmeat, cut into
    bite-size pieces
4 cucumbers, peeled and diced
6 tomatoes, diced
1 bunch green onions, chopped
1 head lettuce, chopped

4 avocados, halved, pitted and
    diced
seasoned salt with onion & garlic
    to taste
2 16-oz. pkgs. shredded Colby
    Jack cheese
Garnish: ranch salad dressing

In a large bowl, toss together all ingredients except cheese and salad
dressing. Divide salad into individual bowls; top with cheese and salad
dressing.

Colorful drinking straws layered with slices of kiwi, banana, strawberries and pineapple are fun fruit skewers for glasses of sparkling soda or frosty lemonade!

Sweet & Salty Pretzel Salad

Serves 16

2 c. pretzels, crushed
1 c. plus 3 T. sugar, divided
1 c. butter, melted
3 8-oz. pkgs. cream cheese, softened
8-oz. container frozen whipped topping, thawed

2 3-oz. pkgs. strawberry gelatin mix
2 c. boiling water
2 10-oz. pkgs. frozen sweetened strawberries, partially thawed

In a bowl, combine crushed pretzels, 3 tablespoons sugar and butter; mix well. Press into a 13"x9" baking pan. Bake at 350 degrees for 8 to 10 minutes, until golden. Let cool completely. Meanwhile, in a separate bowl, combine cream cheese, whipped topping and remaining sugar. Beat with an electric mixer on medium speed for 3 to 5 minutes, until smooth. Spread cream cheese mixture evenly over cooled pretzel crust; refrigerate. In a bowl, combine dry gelatin mixes and water; stir until mixes are dissolved, about 2 minutes. Add strawberries to gelatin mixture; stir well and let stand 10 minutes until partially set. Pour strawberry mixture over cream cheese layer. Cover and chill until ready to serve.

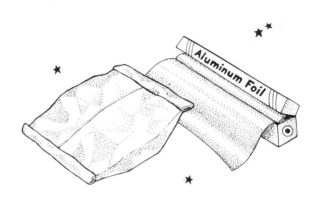

For a side dish that practically cooks itself, fill aluminum foil packets with sliced fresh veggies. Top with seasoning salt and 2 ice cubes, seal and bake at 450 degrees for 20 to 25 minutes.

Overnight Oriental Salad

Serves 10 to 12

3/4 c. oil
1/2 c. sugar
1/2 c. white vinegar
2 3-oz. pkgs. chicken-flavored
   ramen noodles

1 head cabbage, shredded
1 bunch green onions, chopped
1 c. sliced almonds, toasted
1 c. roasted sunflower seeds

Combine oil, sugar, vinegar and seasoning packets from noodles in a
bowl and mix well; cover and refrigerate overnight. Crush noodles in
a large bowl; add cabbage, green onions, almonds and sunflower seeds.
Pour oil mixture over top and toss gently.

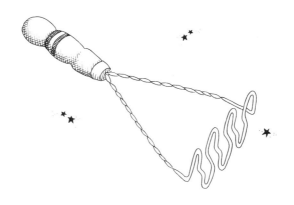

An easy way to crumble ground beef...use a potato masher.
It makes browning so quick & easy.

Pizza Burgers

Makes 2 dozen

2 lbs. ground beef
1/2 green pepper, diced
1 onion, diced
2 T. sugar
26-oz. can spaghetti sauce
  with mushrooms

6-oz. can tomato paste
1 doz. hamburger buns, split
8-oz. pkg. shredded mozzarella
  cheese
1/2 c. grated Parmesan cheese

Brown ground beef with pepper, onion and sugar in a skillet; drain and set aside. Mix spaghetti sauce with tomato paste; stir into beef mixture. Spread on each bun half; sprinkle with cheeses. Arrange on ungreased baking sheets. Bake at 500 degrees for 5 minutes, or until cheese melts.

Freeze chicken breasts or pork chops with their marinades
in airtight containers. By the time it's thawed for cooking,
the meat will have absorbed just enough flavor...so easy!

Dad's Barbecue for a Crowd

Makes about 4 dozen sandwiches

8-1/2 lb. boneless pork roast
6-lb. boneless beef rump roast
4 onions, finely diced
3 T. plus 1 t. Worcestershire sauce
5-1/3 c. catsup
2 qts. plus 3/4 c. water

3-1/3 c. thick & spicy barbecue sauce
1 T. salt
1 t. pepper
1/4 c. white vinegar
4 doz. hamburger buns, split

Place roasts in 2 large stockpots; cover with water. Bring each to a boil over high heat; reduce heat and simmer until very tender, about 3 to 4 hours. Let cool. Shred roasts; measure 10 packed cups pork and 9 packed cups beef. Combine onions, Worcestershire sauce, catsup, water, barbecue sauce, salt and pepper in a saucepan. Heat until boiling; add meats and vinegar. Simmer until mixture reaches desired thickness. Spoon onto buns.

Oh-oh...you forgot to thaw the roast overnight! Before placing the frozen roast in the crock, pour in a cup of warm water. Add an extra 4 hours cooking time on low or 2 hours on high.

Mom's BBQ Beef for a Crowd *Makes 30 to 40 sandwiches*

1 c. onion, chopped
2 T. butter
4 lbs. ground beef
14-oz. bottle catsup
1 c. water
1/2 c. celery, chopped
1/4 c. lemon juice

2 T. cider vinegar
2 T. brown sugar, packed
1 T. Worcestershire sauce
1 T. salt
1 t. dry mustard
30 to 40 sandwich buns, split

In a skillet, sauté onion in butter. Add beef and cook until browned; drain. Spoon beef mixture into a slow cooker; stir in remaining ingredients except buns. Cover and cook on low setting for 3 to 4 hours. Spoon onto buns to serve.

All-day slow cooking works wonders on inexpensive,
less-tender cuts of beef...arm and chuck roast, rump roast,
round steak and stew beef cook up juicy and delicious.

Easy French Dip Sandwiches

Serves 18 to 20

4 lbs. stew beef, cubed
2 onions
4 cloves garlic
2 10-1/2 oz. cans beef broth

4 c. water
4 t. beef bouillon granules
18 to 20 sandwich buns, split

Combine all ingredients except buns in a slow cooker. Cover and cook on low setting for 8 to 10 hours. Discard onions and garlic. Shred beef and spoon onto buns. Serve with beef juices from slow cooker for dipping.

Rolls and buns will drip less when filled with juicy
slow-cooked meat if they're toasted first.

Slow-Cooked Pulled Pork

Makes 12 sandwiches

1 T. oil
3-1/2 to 4-lb. boneless pork
    shoulder roast, tied
10-1/2 oz. can French onion soup
1 c. catsup

1/4 c. cider vinegar
2 T. brown sugar, packed
24 slices Texas toast or
    12 sandwich rolls, split

Heat oil in a skillet over medium heat. Add roast and brown on all sides; remove to a large slow cooker and set aside. Mix soup, catsup, vinegar and brown sugar; pour over roast. Cover and cook on low setting for 8 to 10 hours, until roast is fork-tender. Remove roast to a platter; discard string and let stand for 10 minutes. Shred roast, using 2 forks; return to slow cooker and stir. Spoon meat and sauce onto bread slices or rolls.

Take brunch outdoors! Spread out a quilt on
the picnic table, gather everyone 'round and enjoy
the warm, sunny weather.

Betty's Hot Cheese Toast

Makes 12 to 15 servings

1 c. mayonnaise
2 t. Worcestershire sauce
1/2 t. ranch salad dressing mix
1/4 t. paprika
2 green onions, chopped

2-1/2 oz. pkg. chopped almonds
8-oz. pkg. shredded Cheddar
    cheese
2 T. bacon bits
15 bread slices, halved

Combine all ingredients except bread slices; mix well. Spread on half-slices of bread; arrange slices on a lightly greased baking sheet. Bake for 10 minutes at 400 degrees, until golden. Serve hot.

Need to add a little zing to a soup or stew? Just add a dash of herb-flavored vinegar...a super use for that bottle you brought home from the farmers' market.

Vegetable Beef Soup for 50

8 lbs. boneless beef chuck roast,
  cut into 1/2-inch cubes
1 c. all-purpose flour
1 T. salt
2 t. pepper
1/2 c. oil
4 cloves garlic, minced
2 bay leaves
2 t. dried thyme
6 qts. water
4 15-oz. cans tomato sauce

46-oz. can tomato juice
12 cubes beef bouillon
2 c. pearled barley, uncooked
2 lbs. potatoes, peeled and cubed
1-1/2 lbs. carrots, peeled and
  sliced
1 lb. cabbage, chopped
1 lb. onion, chopped
2 c. fresh or frozen green beans
2 c. fresh or frozen peas

In a very large bowl, toss beef with flour, salt and pepper. Heat oil in a large Dutch oven. Working in batches, brown beef in oil; transfer beef to a large stockpot. Add remaining ingredients except vegetables to beef; bring to a boil. Reduce heat to low; cover and simmer for one hour. Add vegetables to soup; return to a boil. Return heat to low; cover and simmer for an additional 1-1/2 to 2 hours, until vegetables are cooked and beef is tender. Remove bay leaves before serving.

Fill vintage jelly jars with candy corn and set a
tealight inside each one. Their sweet glow will make
the prettiest place settings.

White Chicken Chili

Makes 12 servings

4 boneless, skinless chicken
    breasts
6 15-1/2 oz. cans Great Northern
    beans
2 4-oz. cans chopped green chiles
4 c. chicken broth
2 onions, diced

2 t. ground cumin
1-1/2 t. garlic, minced
1-1/2 t. dried oregano
1/2 t. white pepper
1/4 t. cayenne pepper
24-oz. container sour cream

Place all ingredients except sour cream in a slow cooker; do not drain beans or chiles. Cover and cook on low setting for 6 to 8 hours, until chicken is cooked through. Remove chicken from chili and dice; return to slow cooker. Stir in sour cream just before serving.

Chowders and cream soups are perfect comfort foods.
Make yours extra creamy and rich tasting...simply replace milk
or water in the recipe with an equal amount of evaporated milk.

Boston Clam Chowder

Makes 12 servings

3 c. potatoes, peeled and cubed
1 c. onion, chopped
1 c. celery, chopped
3 6-1/2 oz. cans chopped clams,
    drained and juice reserved
3/4 c. butter

3/4 c. all-purpose flour
1 T. sugar
1 t. salt
1/8 t. pepper
2 c. whole milk
2 c. half-and-half

Place potatoes, onion and celery in a saucepan over medium heat. Add reserved clam juice, setting aside clams. Add enough water to just cover the vegetables. Simmer until tender, about 15 minutes. Do not drain. Meanwhile, melt butter in a heavy large soup pot over medium heat. Add flour, sugar, salt and pepper; blend into a smooth paste. Cook for 5 minutes, stirring often. Add milk and half-and-half; whisk constantly over medium-high heat until smooth and thickened. Stir in potato mixture with cooking liquid. Reduce heat to low; add reserved clams. Simmer for 10 minutes, or until heated through.

For extra-lean ground turkey or beef, pour meat
into a colander after browning. Rinse with hot water...
this washes away most of the remaining fat.

Crowd-Pleasing Chili

Serves 20 to 25

5 lbs. ground beef
5 10-3/4 oz. cans tomato soup
Optional: 5 15-1/2 oz. cans chili
    beans
2 1.35-oz. pkgs. onion soup mix
5 t. garlic, minced

3 T. chili powder
2-1/2 c. water
Garnish: shredded Cheddar
    cheese
saltine crackers or corn chips

Brown ground beef in a Dutch oven over medium heat; drain. Add
remaining ingredients except cheese and crackers or corn chips; simmer
for 1-1/2 hours. Sprinkle with cheese; serve with crackers or corn chips.

Put "eat chocolate" at the top of your list of things to do today.
That way, at least you'll get one thing done.

– Author unknown

Granny's Chocolate Fudge Cookies *Makes 5 to 6 dozen*

2 6-oz. pkgs. semi-sweet
   chocolate chips
1/4 c. butter
14-oz. can sweetened condensed
   milk

1 t. vanilla extract
1 c. all-purpose flour
1 c. chopped nuts

Heat chocolate chips, butter and condensed milk in a large microwave-safe bowl on high setting until melted, stirring every 30 seconds. Add vanilla, flour and nuts; stir well. Drop by teaspoonfuls onto greased baking sheets. Bake at 350 degrees for 7 minutes. Cool on wire racks.

For the best results when baking a large batch of cookies, don't overcrowd the oven. Place no more than two baking sheets in the oven at once, and stagger them so the hot air can circulate around them.

2-4-8 Peanut Butter Cookies

Makes 30 dozen

4 c. butter, softened
4 c. sugar
4 c. brown sugar, packed
8 eggs
4 c. creamy peanut butter

4 t. vanilla extract
8 c. all-purpose flour
4 t. baking soda
2 t. salt

Mix together butter and sugars in a large bowl. Add eggs, one at a time, beating well after each addition. Mix in peanut butter; add vanilla. Combine remaining ingredients in a separate large bowl; gradually add to butter mixture. Drop by teaspoonfuls onto lightly greased baking sheets. Flatten with a fork dipped in sugar. Bake at 350 degrees for 10 minutes.

Super-simple ice cream sandwiches! Place a scoop of softened ice cream on the flat bottom of one side of a cookie. Top with another cookie, press gently. Serve immediately or wrap and freeze for up to one week.

Cinnamon-Sugar Cookies

Makes 8 dozen

1 c. butter, softened
1 c. oil
1 c. sugar
1 c. powdered sugar
2 eggs, beaten
1 t. vanilla extract

4-1/3 c. all-purpose flour
1 t. baking soda
1 t. cream of tartar
1 t. salt
1 t. cinnamon-sugar
Garnish: colored sugar

Blend together butter, oil and sugars in a very large bowl. Add eggs and vanilla; mix well. Add remaining ingredients except garnish. Mix well and roll into one-inch balls. Place on greased baking sheets; flatten with the bottom of a glass dipped in sugar. Sprinkle with colored sugar as desired. Bake at 375 degrees for 10 to 12 minutes.

A large blackboard makes a great bake sale sign. Pull out lots of colorful chalk to jot down the hours you'll be set up, goodie prices and what your fundraiser is for.

Blueberry Drop Cookies

Makes 5 dozen

3/4 c. butter, softened
1 c. sugar
1-1/2 t. lemon zest
2 eggs
2 c. all-purpose flour

2 t. baking powder
1/4 t. salt
Optional: cinnamon to taste
1/2 c. milk
1 c. blueberries

In a large bowl, blend together butter, sugar and zest. Add eggs, one at a time, beating well. In a separate bowl, combine flour, baking powder, salt and cinnamon, if desired. Add flour mixture to butter mixture alternately with milk, beating until smooth. Fold in blueberries. Drop by teaspoonfuls onto greased baking sheets. Bake at 375 degrees for 10 to 12 minutes.

Invite a young friend to bake with you. Whether you're a basic baker or a master chef, you're sure to have fun as you measure, stir and sample together.

Amish Brown Sugar Cake

Serves 12 to 15

16-oz. pkg. brown sugar
3 c. all-purpose flour
2 T. baking soda
1/2 c. butter, softened

2 c. buttermilk
1 egg, beaten
1 t. vanilla extract

Mix together brown sugar, flour and baking soda. In a separate bowl, blend together remaining ingredients; add to dry ingredients. Mix well. Pour into a ungreased 13"x9" baking pan. Bake at 350 degrees for 35 to 45 minutes, until a toothpick inserted in center comes out clean. Spread frosting over cooled cake.

Frosting:

1/2 c. cream cheese, softened
1/4 c. butter
1-1/4 c. powdered sugar

1 t. vanilla extract
1/4 c. chopped pecans

Blend together until smooth.

Jars of clothespins can be found for next to nothing at sales...
glue them to memo boards to secure notes or photos.

Oh, Susannah! Pies

Makes 3 pies;
each pie serves 6 to 8

7-oz. pkg. flaked coconut
1 c. chopped pecans
1/2 c. butter
8-oz. pkg. cream cheese, softened
14-oz. can sweetened condensed
    milk

16-oz. container frozen
    whipped topping, thawed
3 9-inch graham cracker crusts
12-oz. jar caramel topping

Combine coconut, pecans and butter in a saucepan. Cook over low heat until golden; set aside. Mix together cream cheese, condensed milk and whipped topping; divide evenly among pie crusts. Divide coconut mixture; sprinkle evenly over each pie. Drizzle pies with caramel topping; cover pies and freeze. Thaw 15 minutes before serving.

INDEX

INDEX

Our Story

Back in 1984, we were next-door neighbors raising our families in the little town of Delaware, Ohio. Two moms with small children, we were looking for a way to do what we loved and stay home with the kids too. We had always shared a love of home cooking and making memories with family & friends and so, after many a conversation over the backyard fence, **Gooseberry Patch** was born.

We put together our first catalog at our kitchen tables, enlisting the help of our loved ones wherever we could. From that very first mailing, we found an immediate connection with many of our customers and it wasn't long before we began receiving letters, photos and recipes from these new friends. In 1992, we put together our very first cookbook, compiled from hundreds of these recipes and, the rest, as they say, is history.

Hard to believe it's been over 30 years since those kitchen-table days! From that original little **Gooseberry Patch** family, we've grown to include an amazing group of creative folks who love cooking, decorating and creating as much as we do. Today, we're best known for our homestyle, family-friendly cookbooks, now recognized as national bestsellers.

One thing's for sure, we couldn't have done it without our friends all across the country. Each year, we're honored to turn thousands of your recipes into our collectible cookbooks. Our hope is that each book captures the stories and heart of all of you who have shared with us. Whether you've been with us since the beginning or are just discovering us, welcome to the **Gooseberry Patch** family!

Visit our website anytime
www.gooseberrypatch.com

Jo Ann & Vickie

1·800·854·6673